WEIRD AND WONDERFUL SHARKS

written by Annabel Griffin

illustrated by Rose Wilkinson

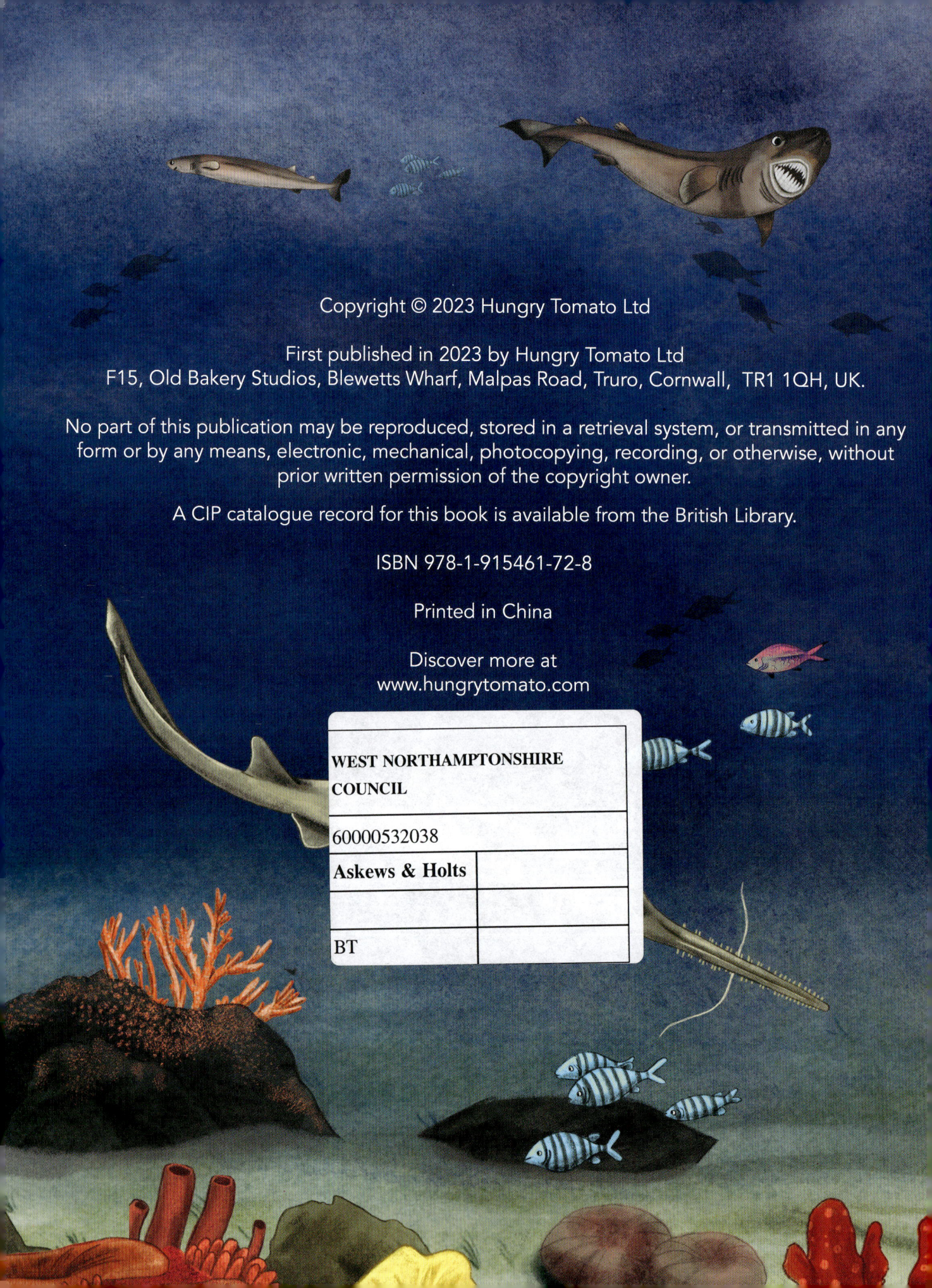

Copyright © 2023 Hungry Tomato Ltd

First published in 2023 by Hungry Tomato Ltd
F15, Old Bakery Studios, Blewetts Wharf, Malpas Road, Truro, Cornwall, TR1 1QH, UK.

A CIP catalogue record for this book is available from the British Library.

ISBN 978-1-915461-72-8

Printed in China

Discover more at
www.hungrytomato.com

CONTENTS

Words in **bold** can be found in the glossary.

WEIRD AND WONDERFUL SHARKS

Some sharks seem really weird, but each and every one is wonderful! Did you know there are over 500 different types? They come in all sorts of shapes, sizes, colours and patterns.

Cookiecutter shark

Terrible teeth

A shark's teeth are its greatest weapon, but not all their teeth are the same. Some have large, **serrated** ones...

... while others are tiny but pointy.

Great white shark tooth

Frilled shark

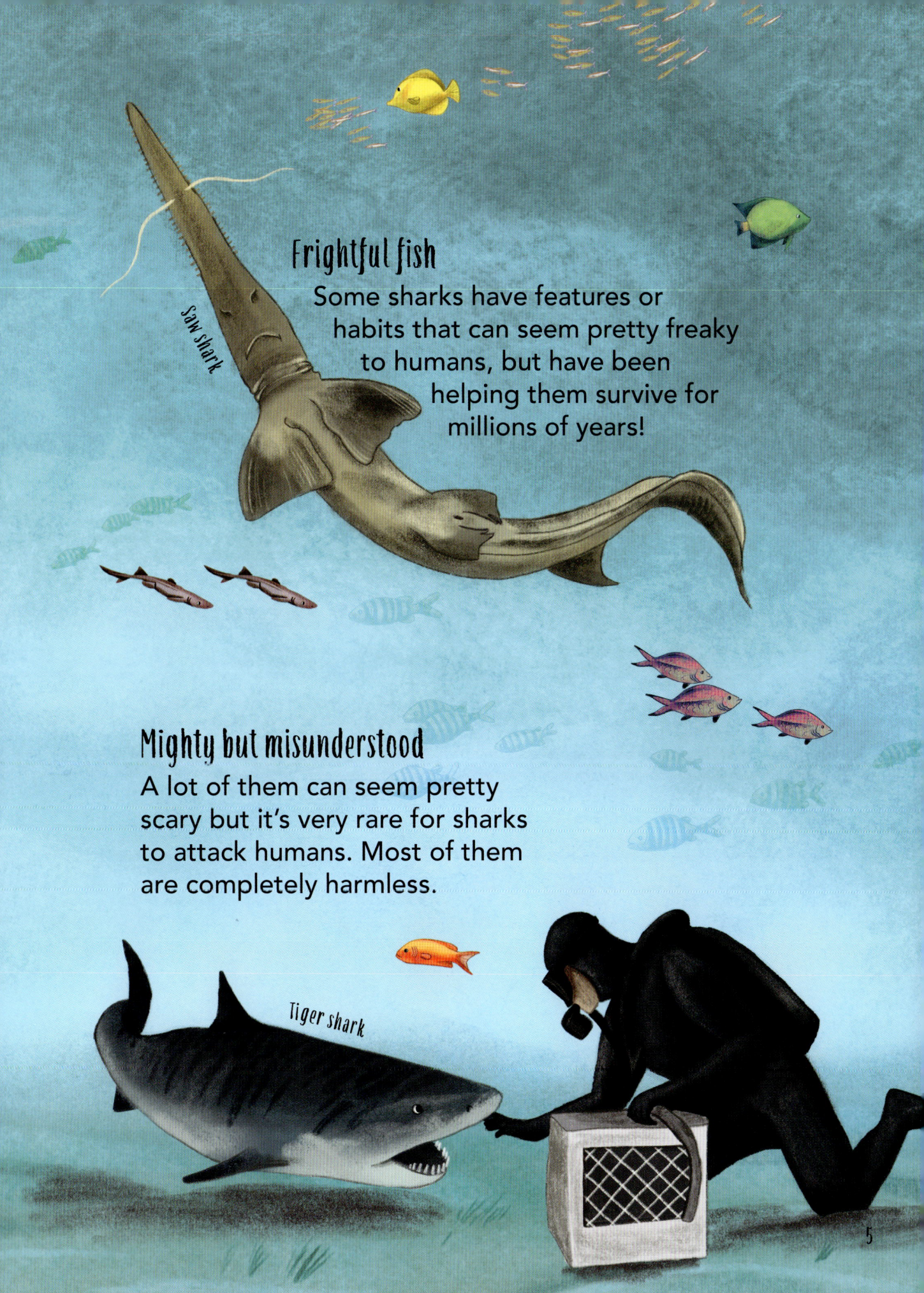

Frightful fish

Some sharks have features or habits that can seem pretty freaky to humans, but have been helping them survive for millions of years!

Saw shark

Mighty but misunderstood

A lot of them can seem pretty scary but it's very rare for sharks to attack humans. Most of them are completely harmless.

Tiger shark

GOBLIN SHARK

These rare sharks have got to be one of the creepiest creatures in the sea!

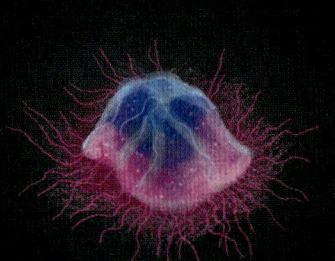

Ancient history

Known as "living fossils", they are the only living members of an ancient family of sharks dating back 125 million years!

Nosey!

The goblin shark's most remarkable feature is its long, pointy **snout.**

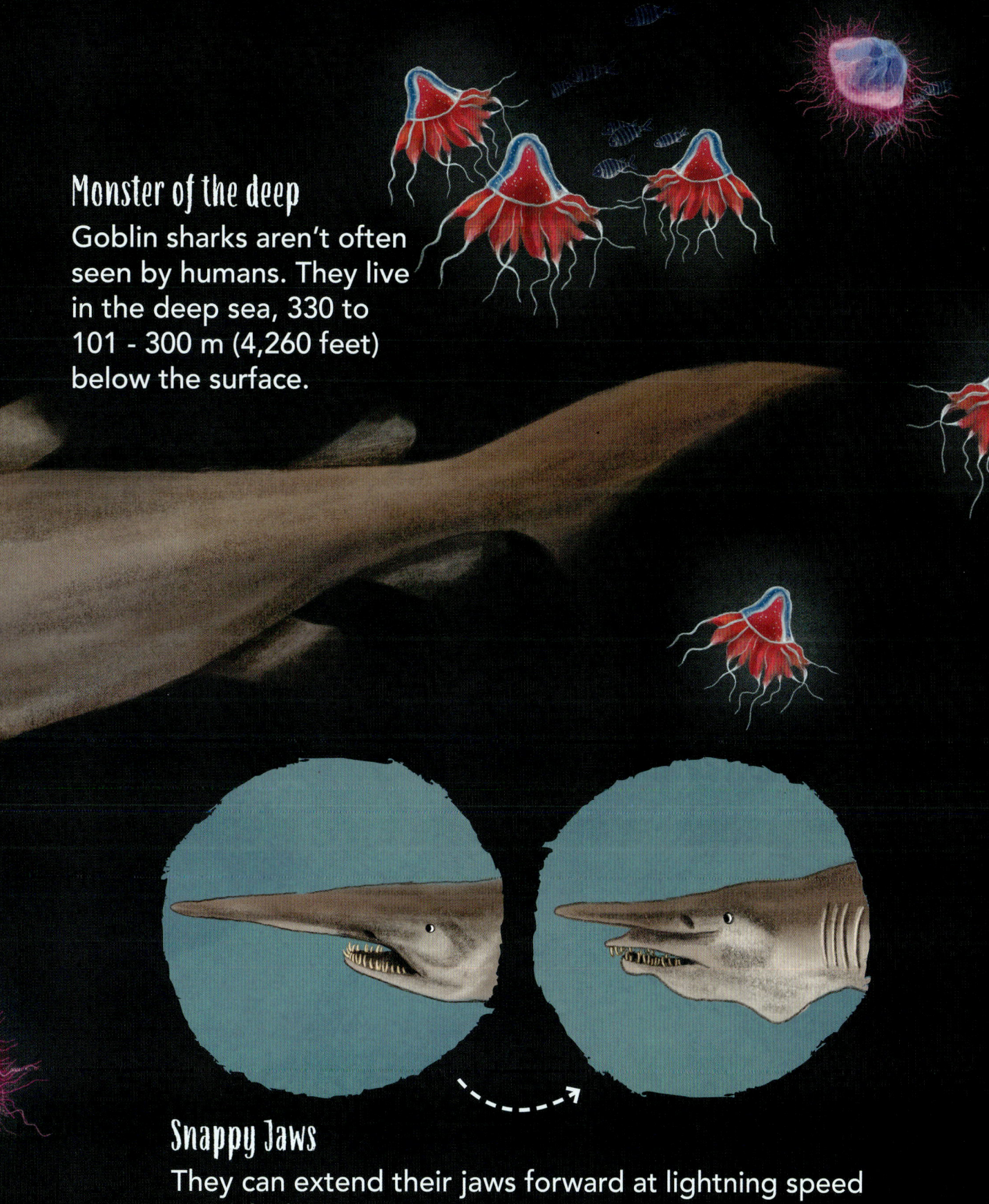

Monster of the deep

Goblin sharks aren't often seen by humans. They live in the deep sea, 330 to 101 - 300 m (4,260 feet) below the surface.

Snappy Jaws

They can extend their jaws forward at lightning speed to grab their **prey**. This makes them look even weirder!

WOBBEGONG

These funny looking sharks are masters of disguise. They spend most of their time on the seabed, pretending to be rocks or coral.

The element of surprise

Instead of going hunting, wobbegong will lie in wait for unsuspecting prey to swim past. Then they pounce!

Funny face

No good disguise is complete without a fake beard! These frilly bits, called *dermal lobes*, also help to attract prey.

Cunning camouflage

There are 12 different types of wobbegong. They all have different patterns that are designed to make them **camouflaged.**

Laying low

Their wide, flat body shape makes it easy to blend in with the seabed.

view from above

SAWSHARK

Sawsharks get their name from their unusual snouts, which look like chainsaws.

Special weapon
Their snouts are lined with teeth around the edge. They use them to slash at their prey.

Little saw
Sawsharks are quite small. The largest they will grow to is 152 cm (5 feet) in length.

mouth

Mistaken identity

Sawsharks can easily be mistaken for *sawfish* because they look very similar, but there are a few differences to spot.

Unlike sawfish, sawsharks have **barbels** on their snouts.

They have **gills** in the side of their necks, while sawfish have theirs on their underside.

HORN SHARK

These slow-moving sharks get their name from the spines on their backs, which look a bit like horns.

Don't touch me!
Their horn-like spines are poisonous and used to protect them from **predators.**

purple sea urchin

Not a strong swimmer
They stay close to the seabed and use their lower fins to crawl along the rocks.

Crunchy snacks
They like to eat hard shellfish.
Eating lots of purple sea urchins
can turn their teeth purple!

See you, sucker!
They use their pig-like snout
to suck food into their mouth.
They have special flat teeth at
the back of their mouth for
crunching down on shellfish.

FRILLED SHARK

With its long, eel-like body and terrifying teeth, this deep-sea creature looks more like a sea serpent than a shark!

Squid dinner

Most of their diet is made up of different types of squid.

Another "living fossil"

Like the goblin shark, frilled sharks have an ancient family history, dating back at least 95 million years. It's thought they also haven't changed much since then!

Gills or frills?

They get their name from their large, frilly gills.

Quite a mouthful!

Their unusual, backward-pointing rows of teeth make it almost impossible for their prey to escape.

COOKIECUTTER SHARK

Watch out! They may be less that 60 cm (2 feet) long, but these freaky looking sharks have a pretty big bite!

Big bite

When it opens its mouth wide, its jaw makes the shape of a circular cookie cutter. Perfect for taking cookie-sized bites!

This sucks!

They use their big lips to suck onto prey, like a plunger. Then, they sink their teeth in and spin around, to cut out a chunk.

Pick on someone your own size!

These sharks go after much larger animals, including dolphins, whales, and other sharks. They're even brave enough to bite a *great white*!

Just a nibble

Cookiecutter sharks leave their victims alive, but with a few chunks missing!

WEIRD SHARK FACTS

Don't roll your eyes at me!

Great white sharks don't have eyelids. When they attack, they roll their eyeballs back into their head to protect them from damage.

Secret siblings

Frilled sharks are so rarely seen that it wasn't until 2009 that scientists discovered there are two different types, the frilled shark and the southern African frilled shark.

Frilled shark

Twisted eggs

Horn sharks lay strange, spiral-shaped eggs that they wedge between rocks on the ocean floor to keep them safe and secure.

Horn shark egg

Puke your guts out!

Sharks can't vomit. Instead, they will sometimes turn their stomach inside out and push it out of their mouth completely to empty and clean it. Eww!

TRUE OR FALSE?

Can you guess which of these facts about sharks are true or false?

Sharks don't have bones

TRUE: They have a skeleton, but it's made from **cartilage** instead of bone. That's the flexible stuff your ears and nose are made from!

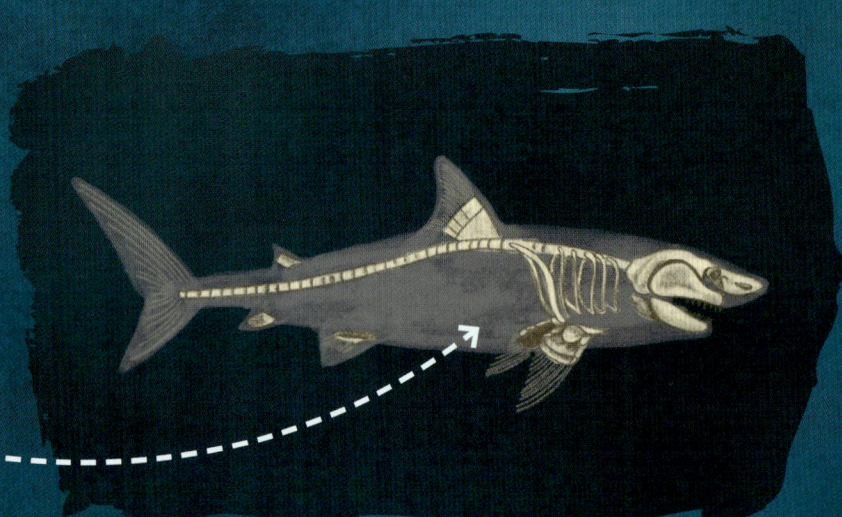

Great white shark skeleton

Huge female tiger shark

Male sharks are bigger than females

FALSE: females are almost always larger.

Sharks can't swim backwards

TRUE: The angle of their fins mean that they can only swim forward.

Great white shark

Sharks have to keep swimming to breathe

FALSE: While this is true for some sharks, including great whites and whale sharks, many, like the wobbegong, can suck water through their gills while sitting still.

Wobbegong

GLOSSARY

barbels

Whisker-like body parts that hang from the jaws of some fish. They are used to help sense food in the water.

camouflage

To look like your surroundings, to help you stay hidden.

cartilage

A flexible material that makes up part of many animals' bodies, including humans. Shark skeletons are made of it.

gills

A body part that sharks, and other fish, use to breathe underwater.

predators

Animals that hunt and kill other animals for food.

prey

An animal that is hunted and killed by other animals for food.

serrated

Sharp, zig-zagged points along the edge of something, like a saw.

snout

A long nose that sticks out from the rest of the head.

INDEX

About the Author

Annabel is a writer and artist based in Cornwall, UK, who writes children's books with a focus on animals and the natural world. She is the author of the *One Planet* series, about Earth and the environment, and *What Can I See in the Wild?*, published by Beetle Books. In her free time, Annabel enjoys drawing, hiking, and gardening. She is never without a good book.

About the Illustrator

Rose is an illustrator, artist and educator from Hereford, UK, now living and working in London. Her mediums of choice are watercolour, gouache, pencil and Procreate.

Picture Credits

(abbreviations: t = top; b = bottom; c = centre; l = left; r = right)

shutterstock: Alessandro De 18cr; Holly Harry 19tr; Frantise Khojdysz 19br; Ivanenko Vladimir 20br; Willyam Bradberry 21c; Dirk van der heide 21br. Unkown: 18br.

Every effort has been made to trace the copyright holders, and we apologise in advance for any unintentional omissions. We would be pleased to insert the appropriate acknowledgments in any subsequent edition of this publication.